A Chekhov Quartet

Russian Theatre Archive

A series of books edited by John Freedman (Moscow), Leon Gitelman (St Petersburg) and Anatoly Smeliansky (Moscow)

This book is part of a series. The publisher will accept continuation orders which may be cancelled at any time and which provide for automatic billing and shipping of each title in the series upon publication. Please write for details.

A Chekhov Quartet

Two Plays
and
Two Short Stories

translated and adapted
for the stage
by
Vera Gottlieb

harwood academic publishers
Australia • China • France • Germany • India • Japan
Luxembourg • Malaysia • The Netherlands • Russia • Singapore
Switzerland • Thailand • United Kingdom • United States

Emmaplein 5
1075 AW Amsterdam
The Netherlands

All enquiries concerning performing rights, both professional and amateur, readings or any other use of this material, should be directed to the translator/adaptor through the publisher.

British Library Cataloguing in Publication Data

Chekhov, A. P.
  Chekhov Quartet: Two Plays and Two Short
  Stories Adapted for the Stage.—
  (Russian Theatre Archive, ISSN 1068-8161; Vol. 8)
  I. Title II. Gottlieb, Vera III. Series
  891.723

  ISBN 3-7186-5778-3 (hardback)
  ISBN 3-7186-5779-1 (softback)

Cover: Chekhov at the intersection of two roads. The signpost reads 'narrative road' and 'dramatic road'. The sash carries the title of Chekhov's play *Ivanov*. Drawing by Dalkevich for the magazine *Oskolky* (*Splinters*), St Petersburg, 1889.

Contents

Introduction to the Series

The Russian Theatre Archive makes available in English the best avant-garde plays from the pre-Revolutionary period to the present day. It features monographs on major playwrights and theatre directors, introductions to previously unknown works, and studies of the main artistic groups and periods.

Plays are presented in performing edition translations, including (where appropriate) musical scores, and instructions for music and dance. Whenever possible the translated texts will be accompanied by videotapes of performances of plays in the original language.

Foreword

In a recent letter to *The Times* Harold Pinter objected to the newspaper's drama critic referring to his one-act plays as 'playlets'. 'While short', Pinter wrote, they remained for him 'plays'.

One sympathizes. Nothing less, it seems, than 'two hours' traffic of our stage' is regarded in this country as serious drama. Consequently the one-act plays of Chekhov, which conquered the amateur theatre in Britain in the first half of this century then burst onto the fringe stage in the sixties with the short plays of Ionesco, Beckett, Simpson and Pinter himself, have still not established themselves in the British professional repertoire.

Partly this is because the ancient genre of 'curtain-raiser' has disappeared from our theatre. Another reason is obviously that to make an evening's entertainment several Chekhov one-acters need to be presented together, as a coherent whole.

It gives me particular pleasure, then, to introduce *A Chekhov Quartet*, because it is precisely that: a coherent programme of Chekhov one-acters that has been tested and works. There are two monologues (really dialogues for one actor with an unspeaking audience) framing two two-handers. Together they create an intimate theatrical experience ranging from high comedy to sombre analysis; and they offer actors an opportunity to display all their powers of invention, characterization, timing, audience control, concentration and finesse.

What more could one ask of any real play?

Patrick Miles

A Note on the Translation and the Adaptation

The primary aim of the translation was to find the internal rhythm and subtext for each character, rather than the search for 'good English'. This internal rhythm is, in any case, 'un-English' in that Russian carries a different musical and emotional structure: the rapid and volatile shift from laughter to tears, or laughter through tears, often appears neurotic or hysterical in English simply because of the differences in emotional range within the respective linguistic conventions. The intention of these translations was therefore to 'translate' the emotional and psychological 'stream of consciousness' or 'association of ideas' within a monologue, rather than translate from one language to another—often an impossibility without distortion. This process involved translation in rehearsal: once the actor had worked through the psychology, subtext, and emotional reality of the character at a given moment, the rhythm made the selection of one word or phrase more organically appropriate than another. The result, I hope, is 'Chekhov in English'—as opposed to 'English Chekhov'—with the rhythm of speech emanating from the emotional range of the character and not from the emotional range of the English language. This 'experiment' in translation through rehearsal is not unique in that the translator is often present at rehearsal; what is different, however, is when director and translator are one and the same, and when the actor—given the range of possibilities of nuance and tone—can decide on the exact word or phrase with the translator.

A debt must, however, be acknowledged to Irene Slatter, Department of Russian, University of Durham, for her expertise in increasing the range of possibilities in meaning, nuance, tone and associations, and for her specialist criticism.

* * * * * * * *

Of these four pieces, two—*Moscow Hamlet* and *Accounts*—were adapted from two of Chekhov's short stories, *V Moskve* (*In Moscow*) and *Razmaznya* (*Nincompoop*). Any reader going back to the original stories will know, as with so many of Chekhov's short stories, that they are inherently dramatic and, essentially, adapt themselves for the stage with very little adjustment. *V Moskve* is written in the first person and readily becomes a monologue; *Razmaznya* is a very 'short' short story with a powerful dynamic between the two characters and yet clearly divergent perspectives, positions, states of mind, rhythms and internal agendas. Adaptation for the stage, however, rendered the sense perhaps more ambivalent than it is on the page: the inarticulateness of a character physically present on stage becomes more potent, and shifts the balance of sympathy; equally, the original story is written in the first person and 'objectivizing' it into a dialogue also alters the balance of sympathy.

Vera Gottlieb

A Chekhov Quartet

A Moscow Hamlet

Swan Song (Calchas)

Accounts

On the Harmfulness of Tobacco

If everyone in this world did all he was capable of on his own plot of land, what a beautiful world it would be!

Chekhov

First of all I'd get my patients into a laughing mood, and only then would I begin to treat them.

Chekhov

I simply want to live, and dream, and hope, and miss nothing.... Life ... is very short, and we must make the most of it.

Yartsev in *Three Years*

The Lord gave us these huge forests, these boundless plains, these vast horizons, and we who live amongst them ought to be real giants.

Lopakhin in *The Cherry Orchard*

A Chekhov Quartet was first produced by Magna Carta Productions at the New End Theatre, London, and opened on 25 January 1990. It was subsequently performed at the Chekhov Theatre, Yalta, for the Chekhov Festival in April 1990, and at the GITIS Theatre, Moscow, with the following cast:

A Moscow Hamlet	Brian Roberts	A Moscow Hamlet
Swan Song (Calchas)	Robert Gordon Brian Roberts	Svetlovidov Nikita
Accounts	Brian Roberts Helene Zumbrunn	The Master The Governess
On the Harmfulness of Tobacco	Robert Gordon	Nyukhin
Director	Vera Gottlieb	
Production and Company Manager	Naomi Lobbenberg	
Stage Manager	Helene Zumbrunn	
Deputy Stage Manager	Ben Payne	

With gratitude to: Tatiana Abramova, Alexander Akhtyrsky, Alexei Bartoshevich, Carol Baugh, Svetlana Garon, Tatiana Shakh-Azizova, Gennady Shalugin, Alexander Svobodin, Valentina Ryapolova, Irene Slatter, Anna Obraztsova, Andrei Tomashevsky and Hilary Wilson.

A Moscow Hamlet

A dramatisation and new translation from Chekhov's short story of 1891, *V. Moskve*, literally translated as *In Moscow*, a parody of Russian 'Hamletism' as exposed originally by Turgenev in his essay *Hamlet and Don Quixote* (1850).

A Moscow Hamlet
A Monologue in One Act

The home of a Moscow Hamlet. The dressing-room. A screen stage right. Tailor's dummy stage left with clothes. Other clothing hangs over the screen. Shoes on the floor. Carpet. The audience is 'the mirror'. As the music for the opening fades down, the light fades up. Music out. Pause in silence and half light, then fade up to full as the Moscow Hamlet enters in a dressing-gown, yawning.

A MOSCOW HAMLET: *(Yawning, exhausted, in a dressing gown).* God, how boring. *(Yawns, stretches).* How boring it all is. Yes. I am a Moscow Hamlet. Yes. Wherever I go, whatever I do—houses, theatres, restaurants, editorial offices—I always say the same thing: 'God, how boring it is, how dreadfully boring!' And everyone sympathises. 'Yes,' they say, 'Yes, indeed, it is terribly boring.'

This goes on all day and every evening and at night, when I lie in bed and ask myself in the darkness why I am so tortured by boredom, I get palpitations in my chest—a restless, uneasy, heavy feeling.

A week ago, in someone's house, I was asking what to do about my boredom when suddenly this stranger—*obviously* not a Moscow man—turns to me irritably and says: 'Well, you take some telephone wires—and hang yourself from the nearest telegraph pole! That's all that's left for you!' (*He gets slowly and moodily dressed throughout the following, wandering between dummy and behind the screen, downstage to the audience, using the audience as mirror*).

Yes. Yes. And in the long sleepless nights I feel on the brink of understanding why I am so bored. So bored. Why? Why? Well, really there are three reasons. Yes. I think so. Three.

First of all—I know absolutely nothing. I did study something, once upon a time, but damn it, is it because I've forgotten all of it or it wasn't worth knowing in the first place, but I seem to keep rediscovering America all the time? I mean, when someone says that Moscow needs a mains sewer—or that whortleberries *don't* grow on trees—I'm amazed! 'Is that so, really?'

I've lived here in Moscow since I was born, but God knows, I don't know how Moscow happened. What's it for? What's the good of it? What's it need? Why? At city council meetings I sit there with everyone else talking about management, but *I* don't know the—well, the square miles or population of Moscow, or the—well, births and deaths, incomings and outgoings. How much trade we do—who do we do it with? …Which city is richer—Moscow or London? And if it's London, then why? Why? God only knows. And if someone asks a question at a council meeting, I start to shake. Yes. I'm the first person to shout: 'Form a committee. Hand it over to a committee'.

I mutter to business men that it's time Moscow opened up trade with China and Persia, but we don't know where China or Persia are—or what they need? I stuff myself all day at Testov's restaurant, but I don't know what I'm stuffing myself for. Yes. I mean, I get a part in a play sometimes, acting, yes, but I don't know what's *in* the play. Or I go to the opera—*The Queen of Spades* but just when the curtain goes up I remember that I've never read Pushkin's story[1]—or if I did, I've forgotten it. Or I write a play, it gets produced, becomes a smash hit, and then I realize that the very same play has already been written by V. Alexandrov, and before him by Fedotov, and before that by Shpazhinsky. I mean, I can't even discuss things properly. When there's a discussion about something I don't know anything about, well, then I simply bluff my way out of it. I put on this sort of sad, sneery face, and take the man by the buttonhole: 'This is *vieux jeu*, my dear fellow', or 'My dear man, you're contradicting yourself! …' Yes. But I have learnt something from our Moscow critics. Yes. I mean, if there's a conversation about theatre or modern drama, say, and I don't understand it, well, I have no difficulty in responding: 'Well, yes, gentlemen. Perhaps… But where is the idea? Where are the ideals?' Or else I sigh: 'O, O, immortal Molière, wherefore art thou?'—and exit gloomily into the next room. Or—there's a certain Danish playwright, I think, called Lope de Vega,[2] and sometimes I really amaze my neighbours at the theatre by whispering: 'I'll let you into a secret: Calderon stole this phrase from Lope de Vega…' And they believe me!… Well, they can go and check!

Yes. I mean, given my utter ignorance, I am quite uncultured. True, I dress fashionably, have my hair done at Theodore's, and this establishment is *tres chic*, yet nonetheless I am *mauvais ton*—an Asiatic. I mean, here I am with a four-hundred rouble inlaid writing desk, pictures, tiger skins, and so on—

and yet the chimney flue is stuffed with a lady's blouse! Or there isn't a

spittoon—so we all spit on the carpet! The whole place smells of roast goose,

my butler looks half-asleep, the kitchen's filthy, and there's dust, cobwebs,

green mould and the smell of cats everywhere. Yes. And there's always

something which isn't working: the chimneys smoke, the lavatory is

draughty, and I have to stop the snow coming into my study by stuffing the

ventilator with a cushion!

Occasionally I take a furnished flat somewhere else and I lie there on the

sofa and reflect on the question of boredom. Next door—on the right—the

German woman lodger fries cutlets on a kerosene stove; in the room to the

left, little ladies drum on the table with beer bottles. I am studying 'life'

there—studying 'furnished flats', and then I concentrate my writing on the

German woman, the little ladies, dirty serviettes! Or I enter into the role of

drunkards and fallen idealists! Yes, or I contemplate the most important

problem: doss-houses *and* the intellectual proletariat! And yet I feel nothing,

and see nothing. I easily get used to the low ceilings, black-beetles, damp,

drunken friends with their dirty boots on my bed. Nothing offends my

aesthetic sense—whether yellow-brown slimy pavements, rubbish tips,

illiterate street signs—ragged beggars. Nothing. I sit, shrivelled like a

hobgoblin on a little sledge, the wind tearing at me from all sides, the driver

blindly whips me with his whip, the scabby horse scarcely trots—but none

of it touches me. None of it matters! It's all of no consequence! People say

Moscow architects have ruined the city—but I don't think their soap-box houses are so bad. People say our museums are poverty-stricken, unscientific, useless. But then, I mean, I don't go to museums. They say there was only one decent art gallery, and now Tretyakov has closed his gallery.[(3)] Well, let him if he wants....

Yes. Well now. My boredom. The second cause is that I think I'm very clever—and extraordinarily important. Entering a house, talking, keeping silent, reciting at a literary soirée, stuffing myself at Testov's, whatever I do is with magnificent aplomb! If I can't utter, then I smile ironically, shrug my shoulders, interrupt. Yes. The truth is that deep down this ignorant, uncultured Asiatic is actually quite content. Yet I pretend to be dissatisfied with everything. The trouble is I do it so well that sometimes I believe it myself. I mean, when there's a comedy on I long to laugh—so I put on a serious face. God forbid if I smiled. I mean, what would people think? And someone behind me laughs. I look round sternly. A wretched lieutenant—a Hamlet like me—looks embarrassed and apologises with 'How cheap! A mere Punch and Judy show'. At the bar in the interval I render my verdict: 'Good Lord, what a play! It's disgusting!'—And back comes the response: 'Yes, a mere Punch and Judy show, but it's got an idea… ?' To which I reply: 'Ha! The theme originated with Lope de Vega. No comparison! But how boring! How indescribably boring!'

But when I really *am* bored, clenching my teeth with suppressed yawns, I put this blissful smile on my face: 'Now this is real! Real pleasure at last!'

Sometimes I long to play the fool, to act in farce—I know comedy helps in these gloomy times—but what would the editors of *The Artist* say? No, God forbid!

Yes, I mean… Yes. Well, I demand honest principles from reviewers… but above all else, I demand that all articles are written by PROFESSORS—or by those who have been exiled to Siberia! I mean, no one who isn't a professor or an exile can have any real talent. Yes. I insist that classical plays can *only* be staged by professors. Absolutely! Yes! And I insist that bit-part actors should know all the literature on Shakespeare before playing a part, yes. I mean, when an actor says, for example, 'Good night, Bernado,' the audience ought to feel that he has read eight volumes of criticism. Yes.

Actually, I get into print regularly. Frequent publication. Actually, only yesterday I went to see the editor of a fat monthly to see if he'll publish my nine-hundred page novel. This editor says to me that he doesn't quite know what to do. 'You see', says he, 'it's so long… so tedious.'

'Ah, yes,' I say, 'Yes. But it's honest.' And this editor, really embarrassed now, says that of course I'm right and of course he'll publish it.

Actually, my girl and women friends are also exceptionally clever and important. They're all alike—I mean, they dress the same, they speak the same, they walk the same. There's this one difference: one has heart- shaped lips while the other has a mouth which smiles like an eel-trap. 'Have you,' says heart-lips, 'have you read Protopopov's latest article? It's a revelation!', says she. And: 'You must agree,' says the eel-trap, 'Ivan Ivanovich Ivanov's passionate convictions are reminiscent of Belinsky![4] Ivan Ivanovich Ivanov is my only hope!'

(*At this point a Moscow Hamlet begins to get undressed, reversing the order and ending dressed in his night clothes as at the opening*).

I confess—there was a *she*. How well I remember our declaration of love! She—heart-lips—sat on the divan. Badly dressed, 'no pretentions', messy hair. So I take her by the waist—and her corset scrunches. So I kiss her cheek—it tastes of salt. She is confused, stunned, awkward. 'O, good heavens, honest principles cannot be combined with such trivia as love! What would Protopopov say? No, 'she says, 'never! Let me go! Let us be friends!'. I reply that I want more than friendship... Shaking her finger archly she says: 'Very well. I'll love you on condition that you keep your flag flying.' And when I hold her in my arms, she mutters: 'Let us fight together... '

So. I live with her. And it is her blouse which is stuffed up the chimney flue; the papers under *her* bed smell from cats; she too bluffs her way out of arguments and exhibitions. She too has to have 'an idea'! And she drinks vodka on the quiet. And when she's ready for bed, she smears sour cream all over her face—to make her look younger! Her kitchen is full of beetles— filthy. When the cook bakes a pie, *she* removes the comb from her hair—and makes a pattern on the crust. Yes. And I mean, when she makes the pastry herself—she licks each and every currant to make them stick! And I run! Run! Run away! Romance goes to the devil, while *she*, so clever, so important, utterly contemptuous, goes around squeaking at everyone: 'He's betrayed his convictions.' I mean… Yes. Tedious. Boring.

Boredom. Yes. The third cause: envy. Boundless, enraged envy. If I'm told that someone's written an interesting article, or that someone's play is a success, that X won a fortune in a lottery, that Y's speech was profound—my eyes start to squint. My eyes close up and I respond: 'Frightfully glad, for his sake. Of course, you do know he was tried for theft in '74.' Yes, and my soul turns to lead. I hate that man and his success! So I say: 'He treats his wife abominably… three mistresses! And he bribes reviewers with free dinners! Altogether he's a complete… yes. I mean, his novel isn't bad but that's because it's plagiarised… Useless… Well, to be honest, I don't actually like his novel…'. What really makes me happy is if someone's play is a flop. Failure. Yes—then I can defend the author: 'No, my dear fellows', I declaim, 'No. There's *something* to the play—literature, perhaps?'

You know, it was me who started all the spiteful, rotten rumours going around Moscow about everyone, anyone, of repute? Someone ought to tell the Mayor that if he actually got us good roads—I'd hate him for it and start a rumour that he was lining his own pockets… Yes. Someone else's achievement disgraces, humiliates, undermines *me*! … So how could I have a social or political conscience? If I ever had one, it was eaten up long ago— by envy.

So here I am, ignorant, uncultured, very clever, excessively important, squinting with envy, a distended liver—yellow, grey. Bald. I wander all over

Moscow, discolouring life, infecting everything with yellow, grey-baldness… 'God, how boring!' I say desperately. 'How ghastly boring!' And I'm infectious—like a virus. A young student has learnt from me. Affectedly running his hands through his hair, he throws his book away and says: 'Words, words, words… God, how boring!' And squinting, his eyes half closed like mine, he announces: 'The professors are giving lectures for famine relief. No doubt they're lining their own pockets.'

I wander around like a shadow. Doing nothing. My liver gets bigger and bigger… Time passes, passes. And I'm getting older, weaker. One day I'll die of influenza and be carted off to the Vagankov cemetery. For two days my friends will remember me and then they'll forget, and my name will fade in silence… Life does not come again. No. if you don't live the days that you have, if you don't live each day, then mark it down as lost… Yes, lost. Lost.

(He begins to exit upstage, then turns as he realises).

And yet I could have learnt anything. I could have studied, loved, culture, trade, agriculture, craft, literature, music, painting, architecture—hygiene. I could have built superb roads in Moscow, started trade with China and Persia, brought down the death-rate, fought back at all the ignorance and corruption and abominations which hold us back from living. I could have been modest, courteous, warm, positive—I could have been truly glad at the success of others for even the smallest achievement is a step towards happiness and truth.

Yes, I could have! I could have! But I am a rotten piece of rag, useless rubbish. I am a Moscow Hamlet. Cart me off to the Vagankov cemetery!

(*He starts to move up stage again, to go back to bed*).

So I'll toss about under the blankets, turning this way and that, unable to sleep, constantly thrashing around with the torment of boredom, and those words will echo and echo in my head:

'You take some telephone wire—and hang yourself on the nearest telegraph pole! That's all that's left for you!'

(*Exit huddled in a dressing gown. Pause. Cross fade music and light*).

Reference notes

(1). Alexander Sergeevich Pushkin (1799–1837), national poet, author of the novel in verse, *Eugene Onegin* (1833), and *Queen of Spades* (both the source of operas by Tchaikovsky, *Eugene Onegin* in 1878, and *The Queen of Spades* in 1890); author of the historical play, *Boris Godunov* (1825), which provided Mussorgsky for the source of his opera (1869); *The Bronze Horseman* (1833); *The Tales of Belkin* (1830); *The Captain's Daughter* (1836); *The History of Pugachev* (1833); a romantic historical epic, *Poltava* (1828), and over 700 shorter poems.

(2). Lope de Vega—Lope Felix de Vega Carpio (1562–1635), Spanish poet, dramatist and novelist, and rivalling Calderon as the greatest of the Spanish Golden Age. Five hundred plays have been credited to him.

(3). This reference was greeted with amusement from the audience in Yalta and Moscow when the production was performed there—a reaction which was lacking from the audience in London: The Tretyakov Gallery, the leading art gallery in Moscow, was long closed 'for repairs' during the perestroika and post-perestroika periods. It reopened in 1994, but was a local and contemporary 'in-joke' in 1990.

(4). Vissarion Grigoryevich Belinsky (1811–48), foremost and influential literary critic and founder of the 'revolutionary-democratic' school.

Swan Song (Calchas)

A new translation and version of Chekhov's own dramatisation of *Lebedinaya pesnya (Kalkhas)*, translated as *Swan Song (Calchas)*, 1887–88, from his short story, *Calchas*, 1886.

Swan Song
(Calchas)
A Dramatic Study in One Act

Characters

VASILY VASILIEVICH SVETLOVIDOV — a comic actor, an old man, 68 years old
NIKITA IVANYCH — a prompter, an old man

The action takes place on the stage of a provincial theatre, at night, after the performance. An empty stage of a provincial theatre of average type. On the right is a row of unpainted doors, crudely constructed, leading to the dressing-rooms. Stage-left and upstage is full of rubbish and litter. Centre-stage is an over-turned stool. It is night. Dark.
Svetlovidov, in the costume of Calchas, comes out of his dressing-room with a candle in his hand, and laughs boisterously.

SVETLOVIDOV: Marvellous! That's really marvellous! —Falling asleep in the dressing-room! The show is over, the theatre's empty, and there I am snoring away without a care in the world! Ach, you stupid old man! You stupid old clown! So you get so pissed you just doze off in your chair! Very clever! Congratulations, you genius! *(Shouts)*. Yegorka! Yegorka, damn you! Petrushka! They're asleep, damn them. Curse them. May they rot in hell!

Yegorka! *(He picks up the stool, sits on it, and puts the candle on the floor).* Not a sound. Only the echo answers. *(Pause).* Just today I gave Yegorka and Petrushka three roubles for looking after me—and now even bloodhounds wouldn't find them. They've left, the bastards, and must have locked up the theatre. *(He turns his head).* Oof! Drunk! My God, the wine and beer I knocked back in honour of my benefit night! My whole body's overheated and I've got twelve tongues spending the night in my mouth... It's disgusting! *(Pause).* It's stupid... Ach, the old idiot gets so pissed that he doesn't even know what he's celebrating!... Oof, my God! My stomach hurts and my head is banging away. I'm shivering all over, and my soul is as dark and cold as a vault. Ach, you clown, you Pagliacci, if you have no pity for my health, then at least spare my old age. *(Pause).* Old age... Ach, you put up a big front, you pretend not to be afraid, but however much you clown around, nonetheless your life is over... 68 years and its already time to say bye-bye, my best regards! You can't get out of it. The bottle is drained dry and there's just a few old dregs left at the bottom. There you are. That's how things are, Vasyusha... Like it or not, its already time to rehearse for the part you play in your coffin. Old mother death is not far off... *(He stares ahead).*

You know, I've been on the stage for 45 years but tonight I'm seeing the theatre as if for the first time... yes, for the first time... You know, its weird, damn it. *(He goes down to the footlights).* Can't see a thing... Well, I can see a bit of the prompter's box... and that other box, the one with reserved on it, and that music-stand... but all the rest is darkness, a black bottomless pit, like a tomb in which death itself lies hidden... Brrr, it's cold. There's draught from out there *(Points to the auditorium)* like from a chimney. Just the place to call up the ghosts! It's eerie, damn it... I've got shivers running down my spine. *(Shouts).* Yegorka! Petrushka! Where are you, you devils? Oi, why am I talking about devils? Oh, my God, stop it! Stop talking like this. And stop getting drunk. After all, you're an old man. It's time to die! People who are 68 spend their time in Church, preparing for Death, while you... Oh, my God... you just use spooky words, you with your drunken gargoyle mug, you in this... in this clown's costume! You just wouldn't see it, would you? Ach, I'll go quickly and change. Oh, it's eerie! I'd die of fear if I stayed here all night! *(He goes towards his dressing-room. At the same time Nikita Ivanych appears from upstage in a white dressing-gown).*

SVETLOVIDOV: *(Seeing Nikita Ivanych, gives a terrified shriek and staggers backwards).* Who are you? Who are you after? Why are you here? *(Stamps his foot).* Who are you?

NIKITA: It's me, sir.

SVETLOVIDOV: Who are you?

NIKITA: *(Slowly goes up to him).* It's me, sir... The prompter, Nikita Ivanych. Vasil Vasilich,[(1)] it's only me, sir.

SVETLOVIDOV: *(He sinks down in exhaustion on the stool, breathing heavily, his whole body trembling).* My God! Who is this? Is it you... you, Nikitushka? W—w—what are you doing here?

NIKITA: I spend the night in the dressing-rooms, Sir, only be so kind—don't tell Alexei Fomych! Don't tell the manager, Sir. I've nowhere else to spend the night, as God is my witness, Sir.

SVETLOVIDOV: So it's only you, Nikitushka... My God, My God. Ah, I had 16 curtain calls, they gave me 3 bouquets of flowers, and many things—they all got quite carried away, but not one single soul woke the drunken old man and took him home. Not a single person. I am an old man, Nikitushka... I am 68 years old... I'm ill. My weak heart is fading *(He leans over the prompter's hand, and weeps).* Don't leave me, Nikitushka. I'm old and feeble. And I'm going to die! It's terrible, terrible...

NIKITA: *(Tenderly and respectfully).* It's time, Vasil Vasilievich, for you to go home, Sir.

SVETLOVIDOV: I won't go! I have no home, no, no, no!

NIKITA: My goodness! So you've forgotten where you live.

SVETLOVIDOV: I won't go there, I won't! I am all alone there... I have no-one, Nikitushka. No family, no old woman, no children. I'm as lonely as the wind on a heath. I'm going to die and there will be nobody to pray for me. I'm frightened on my own. There's no-one to warm me, nobody to show me a little kindness or sympathy... No-one to put this old drunkard to bed. Who do I belong to? Who needs me? Who loves me? Nobody loves me, Nikitushka.

NIKITA: *(Through tears).* The audience loves you, Vasil Vasilievich.

SVETLOVIDOV: The audience—the audience is asleep. They've gone and forgotten about their clown. No. I'm not needed by anybody. No-one loves me. I have neither wife nor children.

NIKITA. So—without a woman, you have no grief! Adam had no grief until Eve came into Paradise.

SVETLOVIDOV: I'm a human being, aren't I? I'm alive, aren't I? There's blood flowing in my veins, not water! I'm a man, Nikitushka—a gentleman. Of good stock! Before I fell into this—this pit, this hole, I served with the military! I was with the artillary! What a fine man I was! Ah, how handsome, how honest, how dashing and courageous I was! Ach, God, where has it all gone? And then, Nikitushka, what kind of an actor was I, eh? (*Having got up, he leans on the prompter's arm*). What's become of it all? Where's it all gone to? My God, I look into this empty black hole and remember everything—everything. This hole has eaten up 45 years of my life—and what a life, Nikitushka! I can look out into the darkness there and I see everything down to the last detail—as clearly as I see your face. Ach, the joy of youth! Confidence, passion, the love of women! Women, Nikitushka!

NIKITA: It is time, Vasil Vasilievich, Sir, for you to sleep.

SVETLOVIDOV: When I was a young actor, full of enthusiasm, I remember a certain women fell in love with me for my acting… Refined, slender like a poplar tree, young, innocent, and as pure and ardent as the summer dawn. The darkest night turned day at the glance of her blue eyes, at her wonderful smile. Oh, the sea's waves may break up on the stones, but the very cliffs, the icefloes, the very icebergs would break on the waves of her curls! I remember how I stood in front of her as I am standing in front of you now. She was more magnificent than ever, and she gave me a look I shan't forget even in the grave... Such affection, like a deep velvety caress. Ah, the brilliance of youth! Drunk with joy I fall on my knees in front of her and beg her to marry me. *(He continues in a cheerless, flat voice).* And she... she says: leave the stage! Le-ave the st-age!... Do you understand? She could love an actor, but be his wife—never! I remember how I played that night... It was a vulgar, slapstick part, and as I played the buffoon I felt as if my eyes were opened. Then I understood that there is no such thing as sacred art. That it's all nonsense and lies. That I—I am a slave. A toy for other people's idleness, a clown, a jester, a buffoon. Then I understood the public. And since then I've never believed in their applause, or bouquets or their enthusiasm... Yes, Nikitushka, they applaud me, they buy my photograph for a rouble, but I am a stranger to them. To them I'm dirt—almost a prostitute. Oh, out of vanity they may seek my acquaintance but they wouldn't debase themselves, they wouldn't stoop so low as to let me marry their sister or daughter. I don't believe them. *(He sinks down on to the stool).* I don't believe.

NIKITA: You look dreadful, Vasil Vasilich. You make even me afraid. Come home, be generous! Come home.

SVETLOVIDOV: From then on I had my suspicions, but those suspicions have cost me dear, Nikitushka. After that story I became... after that girl... I began drifting aimlessly, frittered my life away, not looking ahead. I played endless fools, jesters. I played the clown. And I became a corrupting influence. And yet I had been an artist. Ah, what talent. I wasted my talent, I debased it, I ruined my voice, lost my looks.

This black hole has swallowed me—guzzled me up. I didn't feel it before, but tonight, when I woke up, I looked back and saw all my 68 years behind me. And now all I see is old age. The song has been sung. *(He sobs)*. The song is sung.

NIKITA: Vasil Vasilich! My dear gentleman! Tst, tst. tst. Dear master. Nu, calm down, calm yourself… Ach, goodness. *(He shouts)*. Petrushka! Yegorka!

SVETLOVIDOV: And what talent I had! What power! You can't imagine what delivery—how much feeling and grace *(hits himself on the chest)* in this breast! Ach, I feel as if I could suffocate! No, old man, you listen to me… wait, let me get my breath… here's a bit from *Boris Godunov:*

> Ivan the Terrible pronounced me son.
>
> And from the grave his ghost named me Dimitri.
>
> He stirred up nations to rebel for me
>
> And condemned Godunov to die my victim.
>
> I am Tsarevich. But enough! What shame
>
> To debase myself before the proud Polish woman.[2]

Not bad, eh? *(In a lively tone)*. Here's a bit from *King Lear*. Understand— black sky, rain, thunder—br br br… lightning—dz dz dz slashes the whole sky, and he says:

> Blow, winds and crack your cheeks! rage! blow!
>
> You cataracts and hurricanoes, spout

> Till you have drench'd our steeples, drown'd the cocks!
>
> You sulphurous and thought-executing fires,
>
> Vaunt-couriers to oak-cleaving thunderbolts,
>
> Singe my white head! And thou, all-shaking thunder,
>
> Strike flat the thick rotundity o' the world!
>
> Crack nature's moulds, all germens spill at once
>
> That make ingrateful man![3]

(Impatiently). Quick, the Fool's cue! *(Stamps his foot)*. Give me the Fool's cue quickly! I have no time!

NIKITA: *(Playing the Fool)*. 'O nuncle, court holy-water in a dry house is better than this rain-water out o'door. Good nuncle, in, and ask thy daughters' blessing; here's a night pities neither wise man nor fool.'

SVETLOVIDOV:

> Rumble thy bellyful! Spit, fire! spout, rain!
>
> Nor rain, wind, thunder, fire, are my daughters:
>
> I tax you not, you elements, with unkindness;
>
> I never gave you kingdom, called you children

Ach, what power! Talent! What an artist! Now for something else— something I used to do as a young man. Let's take a piece *(laughs happily)* from *Hamlet*. Well, I'll begin!... But with what? With what? Ah! *(Playing Hamlet)*. 'O! The recorders: let me see one.' *(To Nikita Ivanych)*. 'Why do you go about as if you would drive me into a toil?'

NIKITA: 'O! my lord, if my duty be too bold, my love is too unmannerly.'

SVETLOVIDOV: 'I do not well understand that. Will you play upon this pipe?'

NIKITA: 'My Lord, I cannot '

SVETLOVIDOV: 'I pray you.'

NIKITA: 'Believe me, I cannot.'

SVETLOVIDOV: 'I do beseech you.'

NIKITA: 'I know no touch of it, my lord.'

SVETLOVIDOV: ''Tis as easy as lying; govern these ventages with your finger and thumb, give it breath with your mouth, and it will discourse most eloquent music.'

NIKITA: 'I have not the skill.'

SVETLOVIDOV: 'Why, look you now, how unworthy a thing you make of me. You would play upon me; you would seem to know my stops; you would pluck out the heart of my mystery. Do you think I am easier to be played on than a pipe? Call me what instrument you will, though you can fret me, you cannot play upon me.' [4]

(He bursts out laughing and applauds). Bravo! Encore! Bravo! To hell with old age! There's no such thing as old age! It's all nonsense! Rubbish! Strength is gushing out of all my veins—like a fountain! This is youth—vitality—life! Ach, where there is talent, Nikitushka, there is no old age! You think I'm mad, Nikitushka? You think I've gone off my head? Eh? Ah, wait. Wait a moment. Let me come to myself… Ah, good heavens. Ah, my God… Now. Listen. How tender and subtle! What music! Shush. Quiet!

What is there for you in my name?

It will die, like the mournful sound

Of a wave splashed-out at a distant shore,

Like a night sound in the toneless wood.

On the commemorative page

It will leave a dead trace...[5]

(The sound of doors opening). What's that?

NIKITA: It must be that Petrushka and Yegorka... Talent. Vasil Vasilich! Talent!

SVETLOVIDOV: *(He shouts in the direction of the sound).* Come here, my eagles! *(To Nikita).* Let's get dressed! Ah, there's no such thing as old age! It's all nonsense! Rubbish! *(He laughs cheerfully).* Why are you crying? About old age? Ach, you silly old fool—is that why you're snivelling? Hey, this isn't any good... well, well. Come on, old man, that's just how it is... Why do you look like that? Well, well. *(He embraces him through his tears).* Don't cry! You needn't cry! Where there is art, where there is talent—there is no old age, no loneliness, no illness. Even death itself is half... *(He cries).* No, Nikitushka, our song is already sung. What talent do I have? I'm just a squeezed out lemon. An icicle. A rusty nail. And you? Just an old theatre drudge—a prompter... Let's go. *(They go).* Yes. What talent do I have? In serious plays I'd only be fit to play one of Fortinbras's retinue—and even for that I'm already too old... Yes.... Well.... Nikitushka, do you remember that bit from *Othello*? Eh?

Farewell the tranquil mind; farewell content!

Farewell the plumed troop and the big wars

That make ambition virtue! O, farewell!

Farewell the neighing steed, and the shrill trump,

The spirit-stirring drum, the ear-piercing fife,

The royal banner, and all quality,

Pride, pomp, and circumstance of glorious war![6]

NIKITA: Talent! Ach! Talent!

SVETLOVIDOV: Or how about this!

Away from Moscow! Never to return!

I'll flee this place without a backward glance,

And search the world for some forgotten corner

To nurse my outraged feelings.

Get my carriage!—My carriage![7]

(He goes off with Nikita Ivanych).

(The light fades down slowly).

Reference notes

(1). This is not a typographic error but is retaining the conversational connotation of familiarity in Russian, by dropping the 'y' from Vasily. English audiences are unlikely to understand this distinction, but it does affect the speech rhythm.

(2). From Alexander Pushkin's *Boris Godunov* (1831).

(3). From Shakespeare's *King Lear*, Act III, Sc. ii.

(4). From Shakespeare's *Hamlet*, Act III, Sc. ii.

(5). In Chekhov's original, Svetlovidov quotes from the second canto of Pushkin's narrative poem *Poltava* (1829). In this version, the first six lines of a short poem by Pushkin, written in 1830, is substituted.

(6). From Shakespeare's *Othello*, Act III, Sc. iii.

(7). Chatsky's famous last lines from Alexander Griboyedov's *Woe from Wit* (1822–24), Act IV, Sc. xiv.

Notes

1. Svetlovidov's name is associated with 'svet'—light.

2. Calchas—a character from Offenbach's comic opera *La Belle Hélène*.

3. In a letter of 26 October 1888, Chekhov wrote to the actor Alexander Lensky (who played Svetlovidov), that he had changed the title from *Calchas* to *Swan Song*: 'A long, bitter-sweet, title, but I just can't think of any other, though I've spent a long time trying'.

4. The play was first performed at Korsch's Theatre (a private theatre) with the actor Vladimir Davydov (1849–1925) as Svetlovidov on 19 February 1888, and subsequently by Lensky (1847–1908) once it had been approved by the Theatrical and Literary Committee of the Imperial Theatres.

5. In another letter, dated 14 January 1887, the day Chekhov finished his dramatisation, he wrote: 'It will take 15–20 minues to act. It's the shortest play on earth... It's much better, in general, to write short pieces than long ones; they're less pretentious and they work alright... I wrote the play in an hour and five minutes'.

Accounts

A dramatisation from Chekhov's short story of 1883, *Razmaznya*, literally translated as *Nincompoop*, and variously credited as *Gormless*, and *Day of Reckoning*.

Accounts

Characters

THE MASTER
THE GOVERNESS

The Master's study. He is early middle-aged. Cultured. Kindly. He sits at his desk. Enter the Governess, Yulia Vassilievna. She is young. Timid. Nervous. He ignores her.

SHE: *(Standing a minute).* Excuse me. *(Pause).* Excuse me, Sir. *(He turns from the desk and looks at her).*

HE: Sit down, Yulia Vassilievna. *(She sits).* We must settle our accounts. *(Gets out his account book as she sits nervously).* You probably need the money. You won't ask for it yourself—You are too formal and reserved. So. Our agreement was for thirty. Thirty roubles a month, yes?

(Pause).

SHE: *(Hesitant. Timid).* Not forty?

HE: No. Thirty.

SHE: Oh. Mmm. Mm.

31

HE: I made a note of it. I always pay the governess thirty. Ah. Now. You've been with us—two months…?

SHE: Two months and five days.

HE: No. Two months *exactly*. I made a note of it. Therefore we owe you—sixty roubles. Minus Sunday—nine Sundays. Of course, you didn't work with Kolya on Sundays. You only took him for walks. And three Feast Days…?

SHE: *(Uneasy)*. Mm. Mm.

HE: There were three! For those I must deduct twelve roubles. Four days Kolya was ill and there were no lessons. You only had to look after Mariya. Three days you had toothache and my wife therefore gave you permission not to work after dinner.

SHE: *(Clears her throat nervously)*. Mm. Mm.

HE: Twelve and seven… take away nineteen. Leaving a total of forty-one. Right?

SHE: Mmm.

(Pause. She sniffs, handkerchief to her face. Coughs as if with a cold. He looks at her seriously. Gets up).

HE: Aha. Now. Ah—New Year's Day. New Year's Day you broke a cup and saucer. Deduct two roubles. The cup was worth more—a family heirloom. Ah, well—we let that pass. There's always a price to be paid. However, due to your negligence Kolya, while climbing a tree, tore his jacket—deduct ten roubles. Also *entirely* due to your negligence the maid ran away with

Mariya's boots. *(Sternly)*. You must keep your eyes on everything. It's what we pay you for.

(Pause. She takes a deep breath. He takes a sip of tea).

And so deduct another five. *(He circles her, watching her)*. On the tenth day of January you borrowed from me ten roubles…?

(Pause. Looks at her).

SHE: *(Bewildered)*. I… But… I didn't.

HE: You did. I made a note of it.

SHE: *(Swallows)*. I must have. If you say so.

HE: Take away twenty-seven from forty-one. That leaves fourteen.

SHE: *(Upset. Close to tears)*. I did borrow some money. It was—it was at another time. Three roubles. From your wife. Nothing more.

HE: *(Looks at her)*. So? I haven't got a note of that. Deduct another three from fourteen. That leaves eleven. I have your money here for you, Mademoiselle.

(She rises. He goes to her and counts it into her hand).

Three. Three. Three. *(Pause)*. And one—and one. C'est tout.

SHE: Merci.

HE: Why do you say 'Merci'?

SHE: The money.

HE: *(Furious)*. But I've taken your money from you! Do you understand me? I've robbed you! I've robbed you of everything that's yours. How can you say 'Merci'?

SHE: *(After a pause. Uncertain. Awkward).* Where I was before they didn't give me anything.

HE: *(Facing her. Angry).* Gave you nothing? Not surprising! *(Pause).* I played a trick on you, to try to teach you a lesson. Please try to understand, child. I'm going to give you every kopeck of it. It's here, ready for you in an envelope. Eighty roubles. How can you be so spineless? It's ridiculous. Why didn't you protest? Speak out? How can you live in this world without showing your claws? Can you just be—a lump of—porridge!

(She stands with her head bowed).

SHE: Merci. Merci.

(She exits. He stands looking after her).

HE: Is it so difficult to be strong in this world?

(Fade out).

On The Harmfulness of Tobacco

On the Harmfulness of Tobacco
A Monologue Scene in One Act

Ivan Ivanovich Nyukhin, the husband of his wife. She keeps a music school and girls' boarding school.
The scene is of a platform in the hall of a provincial club.
Nyukhin struts on majestically. He has long side-whiskers, his upper lip is clean-shaven, and he wears an old, worn, tail-coat.
He bows and adjusts his waistcoat.

NYUKHIN: Dear ladies and—well, yes—dear gentlemen. (*Strokes his whiskers*). Somebody suggested to my wife that I should talk—lecture—for charity or something—a topic—of general interest. So. A lecture. Why not? If I have to lecture, I'll lecture. I just don't care.

I, of course, am not a professor and university degrees have left me behind. Nonetheless, for the last thirty years, I've been working—you could even say, non-stop, damaging my health and everything—working on questions which are truly academic. I've done a lot of thinking and—believe it or not—I've put pen to paper and written—well—some learned scientific articles. Well. Not *exactly* learned but what you might call scientific. And incidentally, only the other day I wrote a great opus on *Certain Insects and*

Their Harmful Effects. My daughters liked it very much, particularily the bit about the bedbugs. But I read it again and tore it up. You see, when all's said and done, and whatever you write about it, it does end up as insect powder, doesn't it? We've even got bugs in our piano…

For the text of today's lecture I've—so to speak—chosen certain harmful effects of tobacco on the human being. I myself actually smoke. But the wife said read today's lecture on why tobacco is bad for you—and here I am. Nothing's worth an argument. About tobacco, well—tobacco is tobacco. It's all the same to me. But, dear ladies and gentlemen, I'm asking you to listen to my lecture today with serious regard—or I cannot answer for the consequences. If anyone is frightened, or doesn't like the idea of a serious scientific lecture, then they can stop listening and go. *(Adjusts his waistcoat).*

I would like the doctors in my audience—medical men—to pay attention particularily because my lecture will provide a mine of useful information for them, and this is because nicotine, inspite of its *damaging* effects, may also be used in—medicine! So—if a fly is put in a snuff-box, it will die. Probably from a nervous breakdown. Actually—tobacco is a vegetable. *(Pause).* I think I am right in saying. When I read a lecture my—it—right eye has a habit of twitching, but you needn't pay any attention—its only a nervous disorder. I am a very nervous man, generally speaking, and this eye business began in the year of 1889, on September 13, on the very same day that my wife, so to speak, gave birth to our fourth daughter Varvara. All of my daughters were born on the thirteenth. As a matter of fact *(looks at his watch)* we're running out of time so let's not wander off the point of my lecture.

I think I must tell you, my wife keeps a music school, a private boarding establishment. Well, not exactly a boarding-*school,* but—well—yes. A kind of boarding-school. Between you and me, she—my wife—loves to complain about how poor she is but she has hoarded away quite a sum—forty or fifty thousand, I'd say. As for me, I have neither a kopeck nor even half a kopeck to my soul. —Well, why keep harping on about it?

In the boarding-school I am the housekeeper. I buy the groceries, watch the servants, write up the accounts, make up the copy books, exterminate the bedbugs, take her dog for a walk, catch mice…

Yesterday evening I had the task of handing out flour and butter to the cook because today we were having pancakes. Well, in a word, today—when the pancakes were already cooked—my wife comes in to the kitchen to say: three boarders will not be eating the pancakes because they have swollen glands. So it would seem that we have a number of pancakes to spare. What's to be done with them? At first my wife wants them stored in the larder and then she changes her mind. She ponders and says: 'You eat the pancakes, scarecrow.' She, when she's in a bad mood, talks to me like that: scarecrow, or viper, or Satan. Now how could I be the devil? She's always in a bad mood. And I didn't even eat them properly, I swallowed them whole, and that's because I'm always starving. Yesterday, for example, she didn't give me any dinner. —'You', she says, 'you scarecrow, can do without food…'

However, *(looks at his watch)* we have erred and somewhat strayed from our subject. So—let's press on. Of course, you would now rather have a romantic song or some kind of symphony, or an aria… *(He sings).* 'In the heat of the battle we shall not be overcome…' —I can't remember. Where's that from?… By the way, I forgot to tell you that in my wife's music school, besides being the housekeeper, I am also the mathematics teacher, the teacher of physics, chemistry, geography, history, tonic sol-fa, literature and—everything. She charges extra for dancing, singing and drawing—although the teachers of singing and dancing are also—me! Our music school is to be found in Five Dogs Lane—house No. 13. That is probably why I'm a failure, and why my life is so unfortunate—because I live in house No. 13. And my daughters were born on the 13th of the month, and in the house we have 13 windows… Well—what's the point of talking!

Prospective parents may be interviewed by my wife at any time at home, and if you want the school prospectus, these are obtainable from the porter at 30 kopecks each. *(Takes several prospectuses from his pocket).* And here, if you want, I can let you have some of these. 30 kopecks a copy. Who'd like one? *(Pause).* Nobody wants one? Well… for 20 kopecks. *(Pause).* Annoying. Yes. House No. 13. Nothing works out for me… I've grown old and stupid… Here I am, giving a lecture, apparently quite pleased with myself, when in fact I want to scream at the top of my voice, or run away, anywhere, to the end of the earth. And there is no one to complain to—it makes me want to cry… You'll say: my daughters… What daughters? I talk to them—

and they only laugh… My *wife* has 7 daughters… No, wrong, I think, 6…

(Eagerly). 7! The eldest, Anna, is 27, and the youngest, 17.

Kind gentlemen! *(Looks around him)*. I am an unfortunate. Pathetic and

foolish I may have become, but in fact you see before you the happiest of

fathers. I have to be, actually. I don't dare say anything else. If you only

knew! I've lived with my wife for 33 years and, I might say, the best years of

my life. Or then again I might not. In a word, those years have passed like a

single happy moment—curse them! Curse them all! *(Looks round)*. Anyway,

she hasn't turned up here yet. She isn't here so I can say what I please… I

get very frightened… frightened when she looks at me. Yes, as I was saying:

my daughters have taken a long time finding husbands and that is probably

because they are shy, and because they never see any men. My wife doesn't

want to give parties and never invites anyone for dinner. She is a very mean,

ill-natured shrew, and so nobody ever comes near us but… I can tell you

confidentially *(Approaches the footlights)*…. My wife's daughters can be seen

on high days and holidays at their aunt Natalya Semyonovna's—she's the

one with rheumatism who goes around in a yellow dress with black spots

on it—she looks as if she has black beetles all over her. There are snacks

there. And when my wife is not there, you can… *(Indicates drinking)*.

I might add that I get drunk on one glass and I feel good to my soul and yet

at the same time so sad—I can't describe how sad. Somehow I remember

the years of my youth. I long somehow to run away—more than you can

understand—to run away, escape. *(Carried away)*. To run away, leave everything and run away without looking back... Where? It doesn't matter where... if only I could escape from this rotten, banal, tawdry life—this existence which has made me into a pathetic old fool—the life of an idiot. Escape from that stupid, petty, vicious, nasty, spiteful mean cow—my wife—who has tormented me for 33 years. Escape from the music, from the kitchen, from her money, from all these banalities, vulgar trivialities... and stop somewhere, anywhere, far far away in a field. And stand somewhere like wood—a tree, a post, a scarecrow in a vegetable garden, under the open sky, and watch—all night—the quiet and clear moon, and forget, forget.... Ach, not to remember anything! Ach, how I want to rip off this miserable old coat I got married in 30 years ago... *(Tears off his coat)*.... this one that I'm still wearing to lectures for charity... This is for you! *(Stamps on the coat)*. This is for you! I'm old, poor, a pathetic old man like this waistcoat with its shabby moth-eaten back. *(Shows the back)*.

I don't need anything. I'm above all of that. Past it. I was young once. Intelligent—went to university. Had dreams. Felt like a human being... Now I want nothing. Nothing. Just peace... just peace. *(Looks into the wings and quickly puts on his coat)*.

I'm afraid my wife's standing in the wings... She's arrived and there she is—waiting for me... *(Looks at his watch)*.

My time's up... If she asks you, please, I beg you, tell her that the lecture was... that the scarecrow, meaning me, behaved with dignity. *(Looks to one side and coughs)*. She's looking this way... *(Raises his voice)*. Given the premise that tobacco contains the terrible poison about which I have just been talking, smoking should never under any circumstances be indulged in, and I thus express the hope, so to speak, that my lecture *On the Harmfulness of Tobacco* may have been beneficial to you.

I've said everything. DIXI ET ANIMAM LEVAVI!

(Bows and struts majestically off).

(Blackout).

Notes

1. Nyukhin's name is associated in Russian with the word 'sniffer'—a 'meaningful name' which carries several connations: 'sniffing' snuff; sniffing as a nervous tick, and snivelling.
2. The play, *O vrede tabaka*, has been variously translated as *Smoking Is Bad for You*, *The Evils of Tobacco* (Michael Frayn), and *The Harmfulness of Tobacco*. The literal translation is *On the Harmfulness of Tobacco*.
3. This is the sixth *(final)* version of the play—a monologue in one act—which Chekhov rewrote over a sixteen-year period between 1886–1903. The first version was written in 1886, and intended for the comic actor Leonid Gradov-Sokolov (1845–90); the second was written in 1887; then May 1889; 1890, and finally 1902–3. This re-working of the play clearly demonstrates the seriousness with which Chekhov took a play which he had dismissed earlier as 'an amusing trifle'. Chekhov's dismissiveness about his one-act plays is well-known, but the final version, written after *Three Sisters*, and while he was planning *The Cherry Orchard*, is a tragi-comedy about the tragedy of 'a little man'—and the farce of a man who is not big enough. Several of the farcical hyperboles of the first version are eradicated—such as the original name of Marcellus Nyukhin, which becomes the simpler and common Ivan Nyukhin.